Abraham's Progress
in the
Covenants of God

Glen Burch

ISBN: 978-1-78364-486-5

www.obt.org.uk

****

The Open Bible Trust
Fordland Mount, Upper Basildon,
Reading, RG8 8LU, UK.

Abraham's Progress in the Covenants of God

Contents

Page

Preface

Preface

For Christians schooled in the doctrine of justification by faith, faith in God's promises becomes a bedrock upon which to build. Unfortunately, some believers place so much emphasis on a belief that God will do most of the building, if only we believe, that the edifice does not progress very far and is never quite completed.

Although Abraham's life was very different from ours, there are patterns in it that may be a great help to us today. His life provides examples of faith that should attract every Christian. In fact, he was justified by his faith (Genesis 15:6; Galatians 3:6-9), even as we are. But his life was also marked by deeds, many of which were motivated by his faith in God's promises to him. James' Epistle points out "that his faith and his actions were working together, and his faith was made complete by what he did" (James 2:22).

Although God's promises to us in the current dispensation of grace are different from those

Abraham's Progress in the Covenants of God 7

given to Abraham, even so we are called to a life of good works (Ephesians 2:10). This appears to be a universal principle in the outworking of faith for all of God's families throughout the ages.

What is a Covenant?

What is a Covenant?

Abraham's progress in his faith is set in a dispensation of God marked by covenants. It will prove helpful to review the nature and practices of the ancient covenants, so as to better understand the progress of Abraham's life of faith. The basic idea of a covenant is the uniting in purpose of the covenanters. In addition, the Biblical examples of human covenants in Abraham's time include the goal of peacemaking with real or potential rivals (Abraham and Abimelech – see Genesis 21:22-32) and mutual defence against common enemies (Abraham with the Amorite brothers Mamre, Eshcol and Aner – see Genesis 14:13-16).

At a national level we could liken these covenant aspects with treaty making. However, the treaties we are familiar with in our time typically deal only positively with the issues being resolved. The ancient custom of covenanting differed in that there were both positive and negative elements. These covenants were more realistic in that they recognized the ever-present potential for treachery and covenant breaking. If a nation breaks a treaty today in the name of its own national interests, hardly anyone considers it extraordinary. Similarly the breaking of contracts by corporations or individuals today falls under the civil branch of jurisprudence, rather than the criminal. A breach of contract today is seldom considered to be a moral matter, but it was not so with the ancient covenants.

The Hebrew word for covenant, *b'rith*, is derived from the root *bara'*, which one Hebrew authority suggests has two allied meanings: to eat and to bind.[1] Considering the ancient eastern custom of hospitality and breaking of bread, it is not difficult to see the association of eating and binding. Under such customs one would not usually share bread with an enemy – only with a friend or with a stranger seeking the protection of one's roof. Note the solicitude shown by Lot in

---

[1] *A Hebrew and English Lexicon of the Old Testament*, edited by Brown, Driver and Briggs, page 136.

protecting the strangers who were bound to him by the law of hospitality (Genesis 19:5-8). This root *bara'* is also not far from the idea of a covenant-making feast. The breaking of bread with a rival was a mark of peace (or at least a temporary truce) in ancient times, and this reinforces the positive, or peacemaking aspect of covenants.

The Hebrew word to "make" a covenant literally means to "cut" (*karath*), and this conveys several things. First there is the slaughter of the sacrificial animal that was used both to solemnize the covenant and to provide for the feast after the formalities were completed. It appears that the sacrificed animals were often divided in two, so that the parties to the covenant could pass between the pieces.

> "The men who have violated My covenant and have not fulfilled the terms of the covenant they made before Me, I will treat like the calf they cut in two and then walked between its pieces." (Jeremiah 34:18)

Abraham's Progress in the Covenants of God 13

This divine threat reinforces the thought that a certain grisly fate ought to befall anyone who breaks a solemn covenant. This idea is confirmed by the fact that the same word, whereby covenants were "cut", is used of cutting off heads (David of Goliath in 1 Samuel 17:51), cutting off lives (Genesis 9:11), and cutting off the promises and privileges of the covenants (Genesis 17:14).

Our present day slang "to cut a deal" may derive from this Biblical imagery, but no agreement today begins to approach the solemnity or the possible penalties inherent in the Biblical covenants. Our modern treaties contain no sanctions to compare with threats of isolation or annihilation.

Another aspect of the covenants was the act of sealing it with an oath. Beersheba, which means "well of the oath", got its name from the covenant oath that Abraham and Abimelech swore there (Genesis 21:31). The oath of the covenant very likely contained both a solemn promise to keep the covenant, accompanied by a curse if any party should break it (compare the

Abraham's Progress in the Covenants of God 14

oaths of those Jews who banded together to take Paul's life in Acts 23:12).

The act of covenant making was not accomplished by gathering some words in a document with the parties signing it, as is our custom today. The making of a covenant was both a ritual and an event that often called for symbolic acts and symbolic names to call attention to changed conditions.

Both were present when Abraham and Abimelech covenanted. Abraham offered his adversary seven lambs, apart from his other gifts, as witnesses to his having dug the well that was the source of friction between them (Genesis 21:28-30). He also named that well of contention the Well of the Oath. Both the symbolic deed of providing bleating witnesses and the new name of the well would serve as mnemonics to remind the houses of Abraham and Abimelech that a solemn covenant existed between them.

To summarize, the following elements can be found in connection with covenant-making: a unity of life and purpose, peacemaking and mutual defence, a cutting, a sacrifice, a feast, an oath, a curse, a sign or symbol, and a new name.

God's Covenants with Abraham

God's Covenants with Abraham

Now let us survey God's covenanting with Abraham. It begins with the first account of His revealing Himself to Abram in Genesis 12:1-7. In many translations of this passage there appears to be a misconception about when God spoke these words to him. If the text of 12:1 (notably the verb "said") is translated by the usual rules of Hebrew grammar [2], it would not read "*had* said" but simply "said". The following is my own translation, adapted from Green's *The Interlinear Hebrew-Greek-English Bible* (the Greek *Septuagint* version also agrees with this tense of the verb):

> And Jehovah <u>said</u> to Abram, "Get yourself from your land and from your kin and from

---

[2] See Gesenius' *Hebrew* Grammar (edited and enlarged by E. Kautzsch), section 111, on the use of a grammatical form called the *waw* consecutive imperfect.

your father's house to the land which I will show you."

In other words, this communication followed Terah's death. The seemingly contradictory view that God gave this command to Abram before he arrived in Haran, rather than after, derives from Stephen's speech in Acts.

> "Brothers and fathers, listen to me! The God of glory appeared to our father Abraham while he was still in Mesopotamia, *before he lived in Haran* (my emphasis). 'Leave your country and your people', God said, 'and go to the land I will show you.' So he left the land of the Chaldeans and settled in Haran. After the death of his father, God sent him to this land where you are now living." (Acts 7:2-4)

God's first word to Abram "before he lived in Haran" is not recorded in Genesis – it is Stephen's last sentence, "God sent him", that is recorded in Genesis 12. But Terah appears to have ordered the move to Haran in the Genesis account.

> Terah took his son Abram, his grandson Lot son of Haran, and his daughter-in-law Sarai, the wife of his son Abram, and together they set out from Ur of the Chaldeans to go to Canaan. But when they came to Haran, they settled there. (Genesis 11:31)

The most straightforward explanation would be that the New Testament reveals aspects of what occurred that were held back from the Genesis account. This provides us another instance of the progressive nature of God's revelation over time.

As family patriarch Terah, by custom, would have been in charge of family matters, and it appears he tried to coopt God's promise to Abram for the house of Terah. We may fault Abram for not liberating himself from his father's household, but such is the power of custom. God seems to have accommodated this attempted thwarting of His election of Abram's house but prevented the expedition from going beyond Haran.

The circumstances that caused Terah to dally at Haran are not revealed – perhaps he had no clear idea where the land of promise was located. In Genesis 11:31 it says he purposed to take his entourage to Canaan, but this need not imply that he knew where to find it. Suffice it to say that it was not God's will that he should participate in the promise, so he was held back by divinely supplied means (whatever they were).

We may be inclined to blame Terah for wanting to participate in the Canaan venture, but God seems not to have judged either him or Abram (for not venturing alone from Ur). God knows the dust we are made of and makes allowances (Psalm 103:8-14). Rather than judge the shortcomings of Abram and Terah, we might gain greater edification by trying to understand their circumstances and showing some sympathy for them.

At Terah's death Abram was free to go his own way without interference. God now repeated His promise to him, again on condition that he separate himself from the rest of his family (Sarai excepted, of course). The promise took this form:

"I will make you into a great nation
  and I will bless you;
I will make your name great,
  and you will be a blessing.
I will bless those who bless you,
  and whoever curses you I will curse;
and all peoples on earth
  will be blessed through you."
(Genesis 12:2-3)

Although this command and promise to Abram is not specifically referred to here as a covenant, it does contain the essential terms of what would later be repeated as covenant matters. Even in its embryonic stage, this issue between God and Abram was characterized by some of the covenantal elements. For example, there would be a unity of purpose if Abram consented to God's goal of blessing the earth through him. It would also demand faith on his part, seeing that he and Sarai were childless.

Another covenant element was the mixture of blessing and cursing. While not quite an oath, it certainly bordered on it. Abram's response to God's call was one of faith: he left Haran to follow Him to a land yet to be revealed. However, Abram's obedience to the command was less than perfect, because he permitted Lot to attach himself to the caravan (in my view, the text at 12:4 implies the continued association was at Lot's initiative). A sympathetic mind could find reason enough for this attachment. It may well have been an attachment of the heart. We do not know at what age Lot became orphaned, but it is possible that Lot formed a strong filial relationship with his Uncle Abram. The feelings appear to have been mutual, for later Abram would go to war to rescue Lot's family. Family bonds can be exceedingly strong.

When Abram (and Lot) arrived at Shechem in Canaan, the Lord appeared again and repeated His promise to give him the land.

Abraham's Progress in the Covenants of God 24

The Lord appeared to Abram and said, "To your offspring I will give this land." So he built an altar there to the Lord Who had appeared to him. (Genesis 12:7)

Now the land was already full of Canaanites (verse 6), so this word of the Lord required even more faith on Abram's part. How was he to take possession without expelling all the Canaanites? They probably would not go quietly - would Abram have continual warfare with them until he and his house prevailed?

Except for the war to rescue Lot's household, Abram appears to have been a very peace-loving fellow who avoided confrontation. He seems to have lived peacefully with his neighbours, even to the point of making a covenant with three Amorite brothers. This relationship with Canaanites may seem odd to us in view of their later depravities, but remember that at the time "the sin of the Amorites had not yet reached its full measure" (15:16). Whatever idolatrous beliefs may have been present at the time, there were still some instances of strong moral persuasion to be found in Philistia (20:9), Egypt (12:18), and apparently also in Canaan.

If Abram was in a quandary over dispossessing another people to take his inheritance from God, all the same he seems to have been content to wait for God to reveal the means in His own good time. In fact, that time would be several generations after Abram's lifetime. But he was given more reasons to be content to wait, as we shall see later.

Abram's next encounter with God came after he and Lot went their separate ways (13:7-12). Just as it had been Lot's will to join the exodus from Haran, Abram gave him his choice of whatever portion of the land he preferred. In sending Lot away, Abram had at last complied with the fullness of God's command to separate himself from his father's house. Although Lot was assuredly God-fearing (2 Peter 2:6-9), the promise was to Abram and his descendants. This aspect of the promise was elective on God's part, and therefore unconditional. After Lot's departure, the Lord appeared again to Abram to repeat His promise in even more expansive terms.

> "Lift up your eyes from where you are and look north and south, east and west. All the land that you see I will give to you and your offspring forever. I will make your offspring like the dust of the earth, so that if anyone could count the dust, then your offspring could be counted. Go, walk through the length and breadth of the land, for I am giving it to you." (Genesis 13:14-17)

His land would stretch as far as he could see in all directions. This would mean future conflicts with Lot's descendants, for they would occupy a portion of Abram's Promised Land. Not only would childless Abram become a great nation, as God had previously promised, but now his offspring would be as numerous as the dust. God was now expanding on His promise to Abram, even as Abram had shown himself more faithful to God's word. Another command was added at this point. Previously he had been told to go out of the land of Haran; now he was being told to go into the far corners of a land that would be his and to survey it, so to speak.

In an intervening event in Abram's biography, a confederacy of eastern kings conquered Sodom and took away Lot with his whole household (Genesis 14:8-12). It appears that Abram's covenant with the three Amorite brothers compelled them to go to battle on Abram's part to free Lot's household (14:13-16, 24). This event shows that at least in some cases a covenant between parties would bind together the threads of their lives.

As we shall shortly see, God had this closeness to Himself in mind for Abram's household. When Melchizedek gave God the credit for assuring Abram's success in battle, Abram acknowledged by giving a tenth of the spoils to this priest of God. Furthermore, and contrary to custom, he would keep none of the spoils for himself, lest the king of Sodom be able to say he had made Abram rich (14:18-24). Although Abram's motive here is not explained fully, we might easily conclude that he had trusted in the Lord to deliver him in battle and to rescue Lot. He did not want payment for putting such trust in God. What might have been considered his pay he gave to God's priest, Melchizedek, as an offering to God.

Probably in response to the above-mentioned deeds of Abram, God appeared to him again to reinforce and strengthen their relationship.

> "Do not fear, Abram. I am your shield; your reward will increase greatly." (Genesis 15:1)[3]

God had been and would continue to be his shield in battle, as well as in lesser conflicts. Because Abram had foregone earthly reward, his reward from God would be even greater. At this point Abram expressed some doubts about how

------

[3] My free translation, using as a basis *The Interlinear Hebrew-Greek-English Bible*, Jay Green.

the promise could be fulfilled due to his continued childlessness. But God expanded upon His previous expression of the promise by telling him that his descendants would be as numerous as the stars of heaven. If the dust of the earth was countless, and the stars of heaven were countless, then, in effect, Abram's seed would be doubly so.

At this point we are told that God, discerning the heart of believing Abram, justified him for his faith (15:6). If Abram had his doubts about how he could become so great a nation, he also continued wondering how he would dispossess so many Canaanites to inherit their land.

So God formalized His promises to Abram by initiating a covenant with him. Abram prepared and divided the pieces of the sacrifice, but God put him to sleep so that only He might pass between the pieces. This implied an unbreakable covenant, for the burden was completely on God to fulfill it. In his stupor, Abram saw the twofold vision of the "smoking furnace" and the "burning lamp" (*KJV*), fulfilling the covenant ceremony by passing between the sacrificial pieces (15:8-18).

The furnace represented the bondage through which his descendants would pass while growing into a great nation. The lamp represented God's presence among them ("the glory of the Lord" that filled the tabernacle – Exodus 40:34-35) to lead them out of bondage and back to the land of promise, where they would expel the Canaanites. Now God expanded upon the territorial aspect of the promise.

> "To your descendants I give this land, from the river of Egypt to the great river, the Euphrates – the land of the Kenites, Kenizzites, Kadmonites, Hittites, Perizzites, Rephaites, Amorites, Canaanites, Girgashites and Jebusites." (Genesis 15:18-21)

It is noteworthy that the full reach of that promise has yet to be fulfilled. Although in later generations the twelve tribes came up out of Egypt and took possession of much of the land, they never conquered as far as the Euphrates. God's covenant is unconditional as to the certainty of its fulfillment, but it is conditional as to its timing. One could reason that given a nation of Joshuas and Calebs, they might have possessed it fully at an earlier time. Similarly we can trace a direct relationship between men believing and obeying God and His rewarding them. The Old and New Testaments are quite full of the failures of Abram's seed to believe and obey. While there were some great examples of faith in the line of Abram's descendants, the preponderance leaned toward apostasy and rebellion.

After the passage of more time, it was Sarai's restlessness about the promise of a child that led to her giving her servant Hagar to Abram as a second wife. Although a child would come of this union, he was not the one God had chosen to fulfill the covenant.

Abram would wait another thirteen years after the birth of Hagar's child before the Lord appeared to him again to reinforce His covenant promises.

"I am El Shaddai. Walk before Me and be pure in your pedigree. I will place My covenant between Me and you and will increase you very greatly." (Genesis 17:1-2) [4]

The command to walk before Him conveys the sense of walking righteously in the open, aware of His presence. This would contrast with Adam hiding himself from God after his sin.

The warning to keep his pedigree pure was not just a prohibition about future marriages between Abram's seed and those who were fit to marry into his line. It probably also looked backward at Abram's attempt to hasten God's promise through his union with the Egyptian Hagar. Although their child Ishmael would also receive God's blessings (16:10; 17:20), that child would become a thorn for the child of promise, Isaac, and his descendants. Idolatry was so rampant at this time that God would have to prepare these

---

[4] My free translation, using as a basis *The Interlinear Hebrew-Greek-English Bible*, Jay Green.

unions very carefully, if He was to raise up a whole people to be a holy nation and to serve Him only.

The promise repeated above to increase Abram very greatly (literally "greatly, greatly") uses the figure of speech *epizeuxis* (compare Jesus' use of "verily, verily" throughout John's Gospel - *KJV*). This is akin to a mild form of an oath, one of the hallmarks of covenants. Additionally, God reveals Himself with a new name (another hallmark) – *El Shaddai*, the Almighty All-Bountiful One. As *El Shaddai*, God was reinforcing Abram's faith in His ability to deliver even more than He promised. And to further that faith He gave His chosen couple new names, Abraham and Sarah.

God chose the name Abraham, meaning "father of a multitude", to signify His promise to him in even more expansive terms: now he would be the father of *many* nations (17:4-6). Not only so, but in receiving the new name from God he would become an adopted son of God - no longer a son of Terah. And the terms of the covenant were further expanded. Now the covenant would be with all his succeeding generations. Just as He was Abraham's God, El Shaddai would also be the God of all his descendants. This was to be an "everlasting covenant", like the covenant God had made with the earth after the great flood in Noah's day (9:8-17).

We should understand God's covenant with Abram before this time as unbreakable and everlasting. What God was adding now was the sense of the covenant being renewed between Him and each succeeding generation. It was not to be some ancient agreement that would be referred back to occasionally by later generations. No, they were to live like Abraham and walk before God as Abraham did. It was to be a continually living covenant. The Promised Land would be theirs by personal promise, not merely an inheritance passed down from some dead patriarchs.

Covenant
Cuttings

Covenant Cuttings

At this point God added a condition that was to be followed by Abraham and all his generations after him. The symbolic act of circumcision would become the sign of this covenant in their very bodies (17:10-13). Circumcision was in its own way another form in which the covenant between God and Abraham was cut. Earlier Abram had cut himself off from his father's house; that was the first cutting. The second cutting came with the offering of the animal sacrifices in the formal covenant of Genesis 15.

Now in this third iteration, Abraham was to cut himself off from himself with a more personal offering, one that for him probably bore the mark and shame of mutilation, all prefiguring Christ's offering of Himself as the ultimate covenant offering. The condition of circumcision was binding upon the individual male descendants of Abraham; to disobey meant being cut off from God's covenant promises (17:14).

God's covenant with Abraham was sure and unbreakable, but as far as it applied to his descendants it was breakable with any individual who chose to disobey. In the later history of Abraham's nation, Israel, we observe a dichotomy of the will, with their slipping out of and back into covenant keeping with God. However, the promise in its grand perspective could not be broken. All that God intended to achieve through His covenant with Abraham has and will be fulfilled.

In a subsequent encounter with God, when He was on His way to judge Sodom and Gomorra, Abraham played the role of an advocate and mediator (18:20-33). But first, God finally put a date on His promise of a child (nine months later) and He repeated His promise that all nations would be blessed in him. Then He revealed to Abraham His expectation that he would instruct his children concerning righteous living and the execution of justice (18:19).

Note the contrast between this manner of life incumbent upon Abraham and the judgment God was about to execute against the wicked cities of the plain (19:24-25). Abraham's righteous instruction of his children would be the beginning of the blessings coming upon all nations, for they would first witness the goodness of God in their national manners and mores. Much later revelation, and a later covenant, would show the fullest manner in which this promise to the nations would bear fruit.

> Understand, then, that those who believe are children of Abraham. The Scripture foresaw that God would justify the Gentiles by faith, and announced the gospel in advance to Abraham: "All nations will be blessed through you." So those who have faith are blessed along with Abraham, the man of faith. (Galatians 3:7-9)

Thus the "Gentile" nations of the Acts period were to have a part with Israel in the blessings of the new covenant. Although separation from the idolatrous nations was needful for Israel in their formative years as a nation, God's ultimate purpose was to bring all the nations together in their knowledge of Him. Israel are yet to play a leading role in this conversion of the earth from its reprobate ways.

In his attempt to dissuade God from condemning the righteous in Sodom and Gomorrah with the guilty (perhaps the earliest example of arguing against guilt by association), Abraham exhibited a Christ-like mediation. His own sense of justice must have been reinforced by God's acceding to each of his requests for mercy. One has to wonder whether Abraham believed in his heart that surely there must be at least ten righteous people in the two cities (Genesis 18:32). Or did he dare not ask for a figure less than ten for fear of pressing the issue too far?

Abraham petitioned the Lord five times (a number often associated with mercy in the Bible) and then ceased his mediation. He does seem to have been cognizant of his own personal risk in trying to change the judgment of the Righteous Judge. There is something substitutionary even in this, although not nearly as pronounced as the example of Moses in Exodus 32:9-14,31-32.

Abraham's Final Encounter

Abraham's Final Encounter

In his final meeting with God, Abraham's faith would be tested in the extreme. He was well on in years and had the son promised to him so long before. This would be the fourth cutting that God would command Abraham; that he offer up his only son, his heir and the means of fulfillment of the covenant promises, as a sacrifice to God. In his obedience to God's command, Abraham provided a most powerful type of the ultimate covenant: the Father's offering of His only begotten Son for the sin of the world. It must have been through tears of joy that he spotted the substitutionary ram in the thicket (22:13) and offered him instead of his own son.

There was something of a sign or symbol in this ram of substitution, just as there was significance in the new name Abraham gave to that place: Jehovah-jireh ("Jehovah will provide", *KJV*). Hitherto God had attached blessings and curses to His covenant, but now He would seal His covenant with Abraham, using a great oath:

> "I swear by Myself," declares the Lord, "that because you have done this and have not withheld your son, your only son, I will surely bless you and make your descendants as numerous as the stars in the sky and as the sand on the seashore. Your descendants will take possession of the cities of their enemies, and through your offspring all nations on earth will be blessed, because you have obeyed Me." (Genesis 22:16-18)

The book of Hebrews (6:13-18) makes it clear that this was the highest oath possible, for there is no one greater than God to swear by. The more literal translation used in the *KJV* shows the double use of the figure of speech *polyptoton* ("blessing I will bless", "multiplying I will multiply"), which is used for emphasis to make the promises even more expansive and sure. Add to this the simile of the numerousness of the sand of the seashore, as well as the stars of heaven.

Collectively now Abraham's descendants will be triply numberless (not to be taken literally, of course) – as the dust of the earth, the stars of heaven, and the sand of the sea. The whole of the creation in its three "spheres" (earth, sky and sea) has been used to emphasize how prolific Abraham's promised line would become.

They would also prevail against their enemies. Besides the battles they would win with sword and shield, Abraham's children would also assist God in prevailing against the greater enemy, Satan, by keeping their nation free from the idolatries and perversions of the other nations. Thus they had the potential to become the nation of priests which God later declared under His covenant of law with them:

> "Now if you obey Me fully and keep My covenant, then out of all nations you will be My treasured possession. Although the whole earth is mine, you will be for Me a kingdom of priests and a holy nation." (Exodus 19:5-6)

Although Abraham's descendants seem to have left more bad examples than good ones throughout their history, there were times when a believing remnant provided a good witness to their unbelieving neighbours about the goodness of God. Speaking to the Christian Jews of his day, the Apostle Peter had this to say:

> But you are a chosen people, a royal priesthood, a holy nation, a people belonging to God, that you may declare the praises of Him Who called you out of darkness into His wonderful light. Once you were not a people, but now you are the people of God; once you had not received mercy, but now you have received mercy. Dear friends, I urge you, as aliens and strangers in the world, to abstain from sinful desires which war against your soul. Live such good lives among the pagans that, though they accuse you of doing wrong, they may see your good deeds and glorify God on the day He visits us. (1 Peter 2:9-12)

So it was not until Christ had come and breathed His spirit into those who believed in Him that the nation that would come out of Abraham (through Isaac and Jacob) would fulfill their destiny in bringing blessings to all the nations of the earth. Although he had no more encounters with God after he showed his willingness to offer Isaac as a sacrifice, Abraham continued to obey Him. One of his last deeds was to ensure that his son did not intermarry with the Canaanites (Genesis 24:3), whom a future generation of Abrahamites would drive out of the land of promise. Intermarriage with the enemy would make it extremely difficult, if not impossible, to make unrelenting war against them. It would also make it difficult to resist their unrighteous ways.

After Sarah's death Abraham lived more than thirty years and fathered many more children, thus fulfilling the promise of his fathering many nations. He was content to own only a family burial plot, although God had promised him a large territory that was already filled with many other nations (Genesis 25:1-8). We cannot gather from the Genesis account the full extent to which

Abraham's faith had matured. He had been able to glean from the magnitude of God's promises (and perhaps other revelations through servants like Melchizedek) that God had even grander things in store for those who truly loved Him. Abraham was able to perceive and believe in a land and a city built by God (Hebrews 11:8-10). No wonder, then, that he was content to dwell as a stranger in the land of promise. Furthermore, it was his faith in God's ability to raise Isaac from the dead that sustained him through the ordeal of Genesis 22.

> By faith Abraham, when God tested him, offered Isaac as a sacrifice. He who had received the promises was about to sacrifice his one and only son, even though God had said to him, "It is through Isaac that your offspring will be reckoned." Abraham reasoned that God could raise the dead, and figuratively speaking, he did receive Isaac back from death. (Hebrews 11:17-19)

This was at a time when no one had yet risen from the dead, nor was anyone teaching such a doctrine, as far as we know. If the idea of resurrection was a new revelation to Abraham, then his faith in it must have been profound indeed, for he must have been virtually alone in this belief. We do know from later revelation that Abraham saw Christ's "day".

> "Your father Abraham rejoiced at the thought of seeing My day; he saw it and was glad." (John 8:56)

That "day" was the work that Christ would do in His own time in bringing the children of Abraham to the pinnacle of the covenants. As one of God's first prophets (Genesis 20:7), Abraham may have been granted to "see" these future things through divinely endowed vision. His faith in these things gave him cause to rejoice, we are told. It is further revealed that Abraham was God's friend (Isaiah 41:8), indicating how unified in purpose Abraham had become with God.

Application

Application

Our calling today is one of grace through faith in the risen Saviour. This places us outside of the divine covenants given to Abraham and the people of Israel. However, we can still learn from the life of Abraham and the progress he made in his faith, and there is much for us to emulate in his examples of faith.

Despite his shortcomings, like his reluctance to cut himself off entirely from his family or his attempt to hasten the promise of a son by taking Hagar to wife, he learned and grew stronger in his faith. In his weaker side, we can see a reflection of ourselves if we are completely honest. But we can also draw comfort from the fact that, in spite of stumblings and imperfections, he continued to seek God throughout his life. And God appears not only to have forgiven his faults, but to have rewarded him greatly for the good works by which he proved his faith.

God called Abraham His friend, and no truer Friend might a man find today than He Who gave His life for us, Jesus Christ, the Righteous One sacrificed for the unrighteous.

If Abraham saw Christ's day through types, shadows and visions, how much more have we seen His day to whom God has revealed the secret meanings and nuances of this salvation through His precious word of truth. How much more has God befriended us by revealing to us the fulness of His purpose in calling all men to believe in Him and having "raised us up with Christ and seated us with Him in the heavenly realms in Christ Jesus" (Ephesians 2:6).

Friends reveal their secrets to one another, and how lavishly God has revealed to us His mind and purpose in the aftermath of sending His Son to rescue us from enslavement to sin and death! We are surely not better than Abraham was; God does not love us for the perfection He sees in us. We all need to utter on occasion the confession of Paul, "What a wretched man I am!" (Romans 7:24). Even so, if Abraham with his imperfections could make progress in his faith, then we can take heart that our failings need not keep us from God. We may turn away from Him at times, but He does not turn His back on us.

Our prayer should be that we might also find Abraham's strengths growing in us as we walk with God. Here we have a benefit that Abraham was not gifted with.

> I pray that out of His glorious riches He may strengthen you with power through His spirit in your inner being, so that Christ may dwell in your hearts through faith. And I pray that you, being rooted and established in love, may have power, together with all the saints, to grasp how wide and long and high and deep is the love of Christ, and to know this love that surpasses knowledge – that you may be filled to the measure of all the fullness of God. (Ephesians 3:16-19)

Our shame will be less for the occasional falter and stumble than for failure to take hold of that

Christ-spirit in our lives, enduring with it until the end.

_____

More on Abraham

Abraham and his seed
By William Henry, Michael Penny and Sylvia Penny

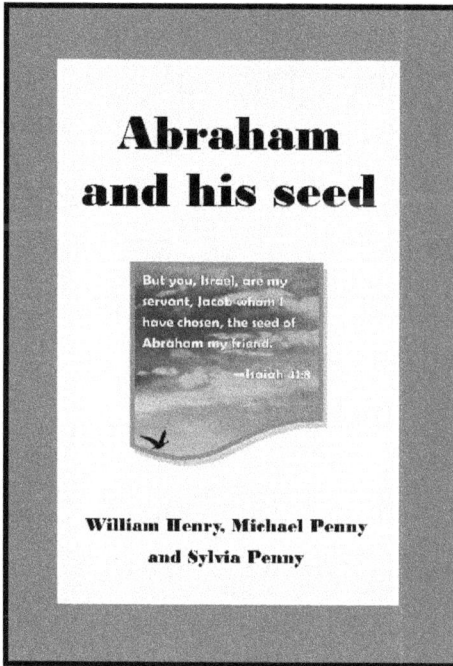

Abraham
and his seed

But you, Israel, are my
servant, Jacob whom I
have chosen, the seed of
Abraham my friend.
—Isaiah 41:8

William Henry, Michael Penny
and Sylvia Penny

In Genesis 12, we read of God's covenant promise to Abraham to make him a great nation, to bless him and to bless all people on earth through him. As we progress through Genesis, this covenant was confirmed with Abraham and with his

Abraham's Progress in the Covenants of God 59

immediate seed, Isaac and Jacob. Later, further promises were made to his subsequent seed, the Twelve Tribes of Israel.

How were these promises to be implemented as the seed of Abraham grew into a nation - a nation that largely failed to follow the Lord faithfully as their father Abraham had done? What does the rest of the Old Testament have to say about the seed of Abraham? Was there any change in the New Testament? Where do those who are not the physical seed of Abraham (i.e. Gentiles) fit into all this?

This book traces the Lord's dealings with Abraham and his seed throughout the Old and New Testaments and considers whether God is still dealing with the seed of Abraham today.

Abraham

By James Poole

The author takes the reader through the life of Abraham. Starting with the call by God, James Poole follows Abraham from Ur of the Chaldees, to Haran, into the Promised Land, onto Egypt and then back to Canaan.

But as well as the geographic journey he also put before the readers the journey of Abraham faith; his justifying faith when he believed God who then considered Abraham righteous. However, as we continue with Abraham we see lapses in his trust of God, but in the end we find a man who has such faith in God that he was willing to sacrifice Isaac, his only son, because he was so convinced that God would have to raise Isaac from the dead if God was to keep his promises.

By Faith Abraham
By W M Henry

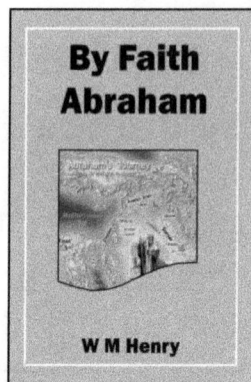

Hebrews chapter 11 records that:

- By faith Abraham when called went, even though he did not know where he was going!
- By faith Abraham made his home in the Promised Land like a stranger!
- By faith Abraham, even though he was past age, became a father!
- By faith Abraham, when tested, offered up Isaac.

William Henry considers each of these with references back to Genesis, giving much helpful background. He concludes the booklet with doctrinal and practical applications which are pertinent and relevant to all who have faith today.

Please note:

Further details of all the books here
can be seen on **www.obt.org.uk**

The can be ordered from the website
and also from

The Open Bible Trust,
Fordland Mount, Upper Basildon,
Reading, RG8 8LU, UK.

They are also available as eBooks
from Amazon and Apple,
and also as KDP paperbacks from
Amazon.

Portraits of the Patriarchs

By William Henry, Andrew Marple, Michael Penny and Sylvia Penny

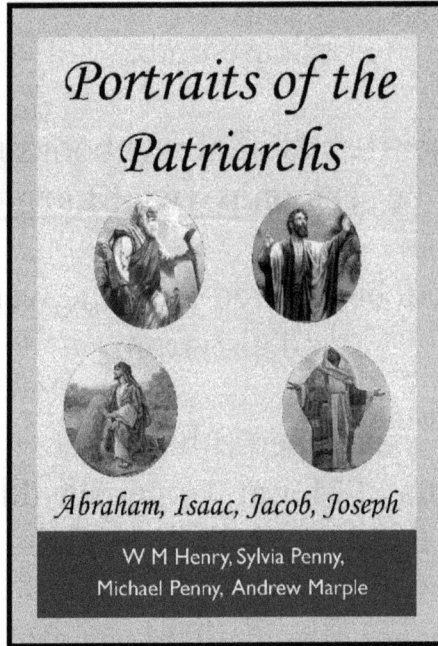

Portraits of the Patriarchs is based on Abraham, Isaac, Jacob and Joseph.

The four authors do an excellent job of not only bringing before us the important issues in the lives of the four patriarchs (i.e. lessons in history). They also, in considering the lives and experiences of Abraham, Isaac, Jacob and Joseph, draw out lessons of faith and practice which are applicable to 21st century Christians.

Abraham's Progress in the Covenants of God 64

About the author

Glen Burch was born in Washington, D.C., in 1947, and is at present enjoying retirement in Virginia where he is a teacher at Grace Bible Church of Hampton Roads. After high school, and his time in the army, he held several positions before becoming a civilian analyst with the U.S. Navy, a position he held for many years.

Also by Glen Burch

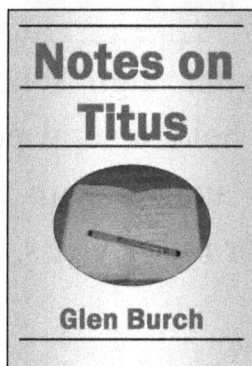

The Mystery of Godliness

Tithing and other gifts

Abraham's Progress in the Covenant of God

Notes on Titus

Search Magazine

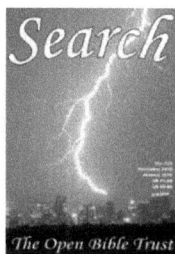

For a free sample of
The Open Bible Trust's magazine Search,
please email

admin@obt.org.uk

or visit

www.obt.org.uk/search

About this book

Abraham's Progress
in the Covenants of God

In short compass the author first takes time to define and explain what a covenant is, before going into the details of the different covenants that God made with Abraham.

The relationship between *covenants* and *cutting* is explained, and a section is devoted to Abraham's final encounter recorded in the Scriptures, that of being asked to sacrifice his only son.

The author shows how Abraham went from strength to strength, concludes with useful applications from his life which will encourage Christians living in the 21st Century.

www.ingramcontent.com/pod-product-compliance
Lightning Source LLC
Chambersburg PA
CBHW060708030426
42337CB00017B/2799